CHRISTMAS

Around the World

RECIPES ~ CUSTOMS

Zu Barnes with Rodney Miles

Bimini
BOOKS

www.BiminiBooks.com

CHRISTMAS Around the World
by Zu Barnes with Rodney Miles

First Edition
Published 2014 by Bimini Books
www.BiminiBooks.com

Dedication

For Clive and Gail, who came to Florida from England on holiday and became my dear of friends. They planted the seed that I should get a passport, even though I was almost 50 years old. My first international stop was in London, England, where I basked in their hospitality and discovered the joys of traveling. Thank you!

—Zu Barnes

Dedication

For my mother, Ronna. Through thick and thin Christmas was always the same for us— amazing! Every year we got to return to the warmth, the family, the thrill of giving... okay the thrill of getting... the food...

They say all true happiness is shared, and my mom showed me Christmas is the best time to share and the spirit can influence the rest of the year, the rest of a worthy life.

And we do it all around the world, so there's hope.

Thanks, mom!

—Rodney (your little gem!)

·

Contents

Introduction

THE CHRISTMAS SEASON is, without a doubt, an extraordinary time of year. Around the world, Yuletide, better known as the 12 Days of Christmas, begins on Christmas Day (December 25) and ends on The Day of Epiphany (January 6.) Yuletide, or Christmastide, eventually became termed, the "Christmas season." The Advent season, observed by the Christian religion, begins on the fourth Sunday before Christmas Day, and ends on Christmas Day. The Advent calendar is popular among many countries and serves as a countdown, often with daily meditations, gifts and excitement, leading up to the most favorite holiday of the year.

Over time, the holiday period in America has expanded to begin in mid-November and end early in January. With approximately 450 billion dollars spent during Christmas, Hanukkah and Kwanzaa, many people complain that Christmas has turned into a commercial nightmare. Despite the protests, these numbers do not deter the zest for a joyful season and families will continue to enjoy the excitement of the holiday. In the spirit of the holiday, we'd like to provide a few new ideas for your consideration!

In our book, *Thanksgiving Around the World and In Your Home*, we suggest that our readers search their "roots," the countries of their ancestors, to discover unique alternatives to traditional foods and harvest celebrations. (Some exceptional recipes in our Thanksgiving book are great for Christmas too!) In *Christmas Around the World*, we urge you join us as we examine prominent Christmas customs and festivities from around the world, and bring you recipes from these countries, which will add a personal meaning to your holiday. There may be foods and traditions that have been in your family for generations and we certainly have no intent to replace those! It's wonderful to consider that, universally, Christmas is a time of joy, of sharing and bringing families and loved ones together. Learning about other countries' foods and customs will enhance the spirit of the season, and we encourage you to read these exciting ideas and embrace the spirit!

Merry Christmas!

Buon Natale from Italy!

Cheers for a Jolly Holiday from

England!

Nollaig Shona from Ireland!

Nollaig Chridheil from Scotland

Joyeux Noel from France!

Feliz Navidad from Mexico!

S Rozhdestvom from Russia!

God Jul from Norway!

G'day and Merry Christmas

from Oz!

Mele Kalikimaka from Hawaii!

Italy

IN ITALY, THE Christmas season lasts between three and four weeks. As the holiday lights and decorations have gained popularity, they are often seen beginning with the Feast of the Immaculate Conception around December 8. Approximately 95% of Italians are Catholics, and a Christmas Novena is prayed daily from December 16 -25, with some observing a 30 day season of prayer, begin on St. Andrew's Day, November 30.

The week before Christmas children will dress up as shepherds, and go throughout the lanes, singing, reciting poetry, and playing Christmas songs on their musical instruments. The presipio, or Italian crèche, is the most prevalent tradition and is seen in homes, churches, and in public areas such as the piazzas.

The mountains of northern Italy provide a gorgeous backdrop for a white Christmas and the ski resorts are geared up for their busy season. The temperatures in Italy in December range from between 20-50 F in the northern regions and 40-60 F in the south. Tourists wishing to visit Italy during December will find that it's less chaotic than during the summer's high season.

Villages, especially in the mountain regions, often use the town square to hold a bonfire on Christmas Eve, where everyone is invited. Viewing the beauty of the classic cities and villages decorated during Christmas, or listening to the Christmas mass in one of old churches is a great reason to visit Italy during December. The one exception to fewer crowds is the Christmas mass at St. Peter's Basilica, where the Pope addresses the throngs of visitors.

Christmas is truly celebrated beginning on Christmas Eve and ending at Epiphany on January 6, which is considered the 12th day of Christmas, the day the Bible indicates the Wise Men presented their gifts to the Baby Jesus. This is the day that most Italians exchange gifts. Father Christmas, or Babbo Natale, has become a common icon and presents are exchanged throughout the twelve-day period.

According to folklore, an ugly but kind witch named Befana was informed by the Three Kings that Jesus was born. She was delayed in visiting the manger and when she finally looked for the Baby Jesus, she missed the Star of Bethlehem and got lost.

On January 5, Epiphany Eve, Befana flies around on her broomstick, visiting every house where children live, on the chance that Jesus might be there. After sliding down the chimneys, she leaves stockings full of treats for the good children, and the bad children get lumps of coal.

On Christmas Eve, it's customary for families to share a meatless dinner, and attending midnight mass. A traditional Christmas Eve meal in southern Italy is the feast of the seven fishes. Panettone, Pandoro and other sweetbreads are served as part of the celebration meal, breaking the 24 hour fast.

After the meal, it's common for everyone to draw a gift from the Urn of Fate, which is a large container that has been filled with wrapped boxes, some of them containing gifts, and some being empty. Children play games and recite poetry, and candles are lighted as prayers are offered around the crèche.

Today, many Italians enjoy stuffed turkey on Christmas Day, similar to Thanksgiving fare in America. The main course for many families is eel, and most meals throughout Italy include pasta in a variety of dishes. In a Calabria tradition, the table remains set even after everyone is finished, because they're inviting Baby Jesus and Madonna join their feast.

If you are of Italian heritage, many customs, traditions, and recipes will enhance your Christmas celebration with a personal flare. We've included a few recipes, but there are vast resources online to help you find ones that will bring a touch of Italy to your home this Christmas.

Eel ~

When it comes to eel, renowned Italian chef Mario Batali, stresses that eel is an essential part of an Italian Christmas Eve celebration. "To most Italians, it would practically be sacrilegious not to have it."

Eel is an oily fish that lends itself well to grilling. Here is a simple recipe that allows for grilling or baking.

Ingredients for grilling ~

2 ½ pounds eel

3 cloves garlic

Salt

Pepper

2 Tablespoons olive oil

1 Tablespoon vinegar

Directions ~

Cut the cleaned eel into 3-inch pieces. Make sure they are washed and dried, and then generously rub on the garlic. Slide the pieces on skewers, and season with salt and pepper. Cover with oil and vinegar and let them marinade with the garlic pieces for about an hour. Grill the eel over a medium flame, turning frequently and basting with the marinade mixture. They should cook for approximately 30 minutes.

Ingredients for baking ~

All of the ingredients above plus ~

Flour

Salt

Oil for frying

Prepare as with grilling except do not put the pieces on a skewer. After marinating, roll the pieces in the flour and fry until they are golden brown and crunchy.

Struffoli ~

An essential sweet treat in the southern and central regions of Italy is struffoli, little balls of fried dough, finished with honey, and a variety of toppings.

Ingredients ~

1 cup all-purpose flour

¼ teaspoon salt

2 large eggs

½ teaspoon lemon or orange zest

Oil for frying

1 cup honey

Optional garnishes ~ Multicolored confetti, candied red and green cherries, pieces of candied fruit, and almond slices.

Directions ~

Mix the flour and the salt in a large bowl, and then add the beaten eggs, and zest, stirring until blended.

On a floured surface, knead the dough for 5 minutes, until it's smooth. More flour many be added if the dough seems sticky. After shaping the dough into a ball, cover and let rest for 30 minutes. Pinch off a portion of the ball and roll it into a rope about ½ inches thick. Slice off ½-inch pieces.

In a large saucepan, pour about two inches of oil and heat to 370, or until a test piece of the struffoli dough turns brown. Place the dough into the hot oil in batches. Turn with a spoon for one-two minutes, until the struffoli are brown and crisp. Remove the cooked balls and place on paper towels to drain.

Warm the honey in a large pan, and then remove from the heat. Pour the cooked struffoli into the pan of warm honey and stir well. The coated balls can be arranged into a ring, or simply piled on a large plate. Use the optional garnishes to sprinkle over the struffoli and serve. The dessert will be good at room temperature for 3 days, if it lasts that long!

"Buon Natale!"

England

HOLIDAYS IN ENGLAND are often referred to as "Bank Holidays." In addition to Christmas Day on December 25, Boxing Day on December 26 is a day to continue to holiday celebration for citizens of the United Kingdom. Shoppers enjoy the after Christmas sales, which often begin on Boxing Day.

The term "boxing" has several different possible origins, none of which is the sport of boxing. All of these customs are valid and the concept of "Boxing Day" can refer to any of the traditions.

~Brits refer to a Christmas gift as a Christmas "box."

~Servants received a day off and often got a "Christmas Box" from their master. In turn, they would reunite with their families and present "Christmas Boxes" to them.

~On Christmas Day, churches would provide a collection box for the poor, which was opened and distributed the day after Christmas.

~Large sailing ships would carry a sealed box of money on board for good luck. When the ship safely returned, the box was given to a local priest to share with the less fortunate at Christmastime.

Boxing Day is also a hunting day and often residents meet in village squares with their dogs.

In the 1840's the first Christmas card was mailed in England. Many cards that encompass the billion cards posted in UK are printed and sold to aid British charities.

That same decade, Prince Albert, husband of Queen Victoria, introduced a Christmas tree into the Royal Household, making it popular throughout the country. Every year since 1947, Norway has sent a large tree, which is to commemorate the Anglo-Norwegian allies during WWII. It is decorated and placed in Trafalgar Square in London for all to enjoy.

Father Christmas, originally known as "Sir Christmas" or "Old Winter," was dressed in a green robe, to signify the return of spring after the old English midwinter festival. He was not associated with gift given, but simply went door-to-door, visiting with families to bring cheer. Beginning in the 19th century, Father Christmas role evolved into the jolly old man who brings gifts to children who leave stockings by the fireplace or bags by their beds. Children would write letters to Father Christmas to let him know what they want, then throw the envelopes in the fireplace, where the smoke will carry the messages up the chimney. Of course, on Christmas Eve, a glass of sherry was left for

Father Christmas, along with carrots for the reindeer.

Christmas crackers are pulled at the table during the Christmas Day feast.

In 1846, a London baker devised a colored paper tube, with the ends twisted. When pulled, it makes a "crack" and the contents of toys, hats, riddles or other trinkets spill out. Many snacks are on display to eat between meals. Nuts in shells, dates, figs, chocolates, fruit like Satsuma, tangerines or clementine are just a few of the English's favorites.

Christmas dinner usually contains two meat dishes. Turkey, beef or pork roast, goose or lamb are often featured. Vegetables often include roasted parsnips, potatoes, Yorkshire pudding, stuffing made with sage, onion or chestnuts. Desserts consist of Christmas pudding, heavily laden with fruit and often laced with whisky or brandy, which is set alight at the table.

It might also be accompanied by a white sauce or custard, whipped cream or brandy butter. Hot or cold mince pies, Dundee cake and Trifle are also favorite desserts.

In the afternoon on Christmas Day, everyone gathers around the television to watch the Royal Christmas Message.

The traditional broadcast began in 1932 with by King George V. Since Queen Elizabeth II has read the message since 1952, it is also called The

Queen's Christmas Message, and is broadcast on television, radio, and the Internet via various providers. Previous year's messages can be read or view on several websites.

*Thanks to my dear friends, Clive and Gail Windley of Margate, Kent, England for their hospitality whilst I visited England, and their personal insights into this chapter on English traditions.

Mince Pie ~

Traditional mice pies are a sure sign of the Christmas season in the UK. Served as a small tart, any tea party, office gathering or evening soiree is certain to have a supply of pies. Eating a pie every day beginning 1 December is considered to bring you good luck!

Ingredients ~

1 ¼ pounds beef or leftover roast

¼ pound suet

6 apples

1 cup currants or raisins

½ cup granulated sugar

½ cup dark brown sugar

¼ teaspoon black pepper

½ teaspoon salt

2 teaspoons ground cinnamon

1 teaspoon ground clove

2 teaspoons ground nutmeg

¼ cup brandy

2 cups apple cider or juice

4 Prepared piecrusts for regular 2 regular size
pies

OR

Cut prepared pie or filo dough into circles slightly larger than muffin hole for 24 2-inch tarts or 12 4-inch tarts.

3 tablespoons soften or melted butter

Directions ~

If beef is not cooked, slowly stew for 2-3 hours until tender. In the last ½ hour, add the suet.

Chop the cooked beef and suet into tiny pieces.

Peel and chop apples for 3 cups small pieces.

In a large bowl, add meat/suet mixture, raisins, apples, all the sugars and spices, brandy, and apple juice.

Prepare the piecrusts.

Preheat oven to 400 degrees F.

For full pies, line the pie tin with pastry; add half the meat mixture to each, then place the second pastry on top, pinching the edges to seat. Make a design with at least two holes into the top crust for the steam. Brush on butter if desired. Bake for about 1 hour.

For smaller pies, place the circular pastry into each tart hole; add about 1-2 teaspoons of the meat mixture. Using additional pastry, use a cookie cutter to cut a star or other shape and place it on top of the meat, pinching sides. If desired, brush on butter and sprinkle a little sugar on the top, then bake for about 10-15 minutes.

With either pie, place on wire rack and serve warm or at room temperature. Refrigerate unused pie. Tarts freeze well.

Traditional Christmas Goose ~

The idea of serving a roasted goose for Christmas dinner brings a hint of Victorian England to a holiday feast. Here is a basic recipe for cooking a goose, in which the cavity flavors are removed and not eaten. If you desire, you can add a chestnut or other stuffing, which you can enjoy with the finished goose.

Ingredients ~

1 10 -12 pound goose

1 teaspoon salt

½ teaspoon pepper

1 Sprig of thyme

3 pieces of parsley

3 apples, cut into quarters

3 onions cut into quarters

2 stalks celery, cut into 1-inch pieces

5 cups water

6 Tablespoons flour

Beef broth

Directions ~

Remove giblets from goose, cut off any excess neck, and set these aside. (Directions for giblet gravy are included at the end of this recipe.) Cut off any extra fat from the tail. Combine salt and pepper and use your hand to rub it inside the cavity of the goose. In a bowl, mix the thyme, parsley, quartered apples, quartered onion, and the celery pieces. Insert this mixture into the goose cavity and use a skewer and twine to close the opening. Fold wings back. Place goose in pan with the breast down. Use a knife or fork to prick the goose skin.

Place in a preheated oven (500 degrees) and roast for 30 minutes. Lower temperature to 400 degrees, and continue cooking for 30 minutes. Turn breast side up and prick goose skin. Roast for 1 hour, still at 400 degrees. Remove drippings from goose roaster and put aside. Prick goose skin again. Add 2 cups water in pan. Cook for 1 ½ hours more. Remove liquid from pan and put aside. Rest goose for 30 minutes. Remove trussing and discard items used for stuffing.

Giblet Gravy ~

Place neck, giblets and 3 cups of water in a medium saucepan and simmer for about 10 minutes. Remove liver and put aside. Lower heat and cook for 1 ½ hours. Drain liquid and throw away the neck. Chop the liver and giblets into small pieces. Use 6 Tablespoons of the fat from the drippings and heat in saucepan. Whisk in 3 Tablespoons of flour and simmer 3-4 minutes. Combine drippings with beef broth to make 3 cups, and then add this to the pan. Heat at medium-high until thick, and add chopped liver and giblets. Salt and pepper, and continue to cook over low heat.

"Cheers for a Jolly Holiday!"

Ireland

MANY OF IRELAND'S Christmas traditions date back to the period when Gaelic customs and the country's religion were being repressed, and yet many have continued to be respected and practiced in current times. The vast majority of Irish are Catholic and midnight mass on Christmas Eve is a time to reflect on Christ, rather than the fun often associated with Christmas. Christmas in Ireland begins on Christmas Eve and is celebrated until January 6, which is the feast of the Epiphany and denoted as "Little Christmas."

The first day on the Advent Calendar is the time to put up decorations. Christmas trees are adorned with ornaments and a star or angel is used as a topper. Santa Claus dresses a bit differently wearing a green suit and often a green top hat.

He may be depicted with a rainbow and pot of gold or shamrocks. As with other countries traditions, Santa arrives through the chimney, leaving gifts around the Christmas tree and in stockings. In addition to the stockings, families put candy canes, elves and other winter decorations on the fireplace mantle to encourage a cheerful holiday ambiance.

Throughout Ireland, people place a lighted candle in their windows, partly for decorative purposes but mainly as a symbol to invite the shelter seeking Joseph and Mary to a warm home. During historic periods of strict religious sanctions, priests were not permitted to perform mass, but a candle in a window signified a safe place to gather for the sacrament. Another part of the custom is that the youngest member of the family should lite the candle and it should only be tradition is that the candle should be lit by the youngest member of the household and only be snuffed by a girl named Mary.

On Christmas Eve, after the family has their evening meal, the table is set once more as a welcome for Mary and Joseph or anyone in need of shelter. A whole loaf of bread containing caraway seeds and raisins, a pitcher of milk is left for the weary travelers.

Ireland, part of the United Kingdom, also celebrates Boxing Day, and there it is more commonly known as "St. Stephen's Day." St. Stephen is thought to be the first Christian martyr and his belief in Jesus caused his death by stoning around 33 AD. Irish legend has it that St. Stephen's hiding place was revealed by a wren, and people began the Day of the Wren, where wrens were stoned to death. This barbaric custom was discontinued in the early 1900s but the name is concurrent with the day following Christmas day.

Included below are some traditional Irish recipes, which you will enjoy.

Garlic Stuffed Leg of Lamb ~

Ingredients ~

2 ½ pounds boneless ½ leg of lamb

Bunch of flat leaf parsley, chopped

3 large cloves garlic, sliced

2 ½ ounce cubed pancetta or bacon

3 Tablespoons extra virgin olive oil

Sea salt and pepper

5 ounces red wine

3 ½ ounces beef stock

2 Tablespoons chilled butter, cut into small pieces

Directions ~

Preheat the oven to 350°F. Place leg of lamb with the skin side down and the joint lays flat.

Cover the lamb with the garlic, pancetta and parsley. Pour on the olive oil and salt/pepper. Return lamb to folded position and tie with kitchen twine, and put in a large roasting pan. Cook for 1 hour to 1.25 hours, and then allow the covered lamb to let rest for 10 minutes. As soon as the sauce is ready, serve the sliced lamb while it is still hot.

Remove the fat and put the roasting pan on the stop top, on medium heat. Add the red wine, while scraping the bottom of the pan, reducing to a thick glaze. Pour in the stock, stirring and reduce to half the liquid. Use a strainer to pour the liquid into a saucepan. Add butter and gently stir until the butter melts.

Cheese and Pear Tart ~

(Vegetarian friendly)

Ingredients ~

8 ounces puff pastry

4 ounces British or Irish crumbly blue cheese

1 ounce walnuts, lightly crushed

2 ripe pears, peeled, cored, sliced

4 ounces melted butter

Pinch of salt and pepper

Directions ~

Preheat oven to 350°F.

Use four tart dishes that are 4" in diameter.
Line the bottom of the dishes with premade puff

pastry. Prick the bottom of the pastry to provide air.

Crumble up the cheese, separate it into four portions and place a portion in each dish. Put the walnuts on the cheese.

Make a circle with the pears over the walnuts.

Use melted butter, brushing it over the pears. Bake approximately 20-30 minutes, when the pastry rises and is light brown.

Add additional walnuts on the top, if desired.

Classic Irish Coffee ~

Ingredients ~

1 cup fresh brewed coffee

1 teaspoon brown sugar

1½ ounces of Irish whiskey

Whipped cream

Directions ~

Brew your favorite coffee and stir in the sugar and whiskey. (For larger mugs of coffee, you might need to increase the amount of whiskey.) Add a dollop of whipped cream on the top, and you've made an "iontach" (Irish Gaelic for wonderful/marvelous) cup of Irish coffee recipe.

"Nollaig Shona!"

Scotland

HAVING VISITED SCOTLAND, I find it to be a country filled with rich history and extraordinary beauty. The residents are generous and their hospitality is unequaled. Christmas in Scotland is a magical season, filled with lush decorations and a spirit of plentiful giving, which is intriguing since Christmas celebration was banned for years and discouraged by the church for almost 400 years!

Oliver Cromwell, the ruler of the United Kingdom, passed the law in 1647. Although the ban was lift after 15 years, the Presbyterian Church in Scotland rejected Christmas celebrations and citizens who ignored the edit were punished. The church's influence decreased around the 1980's and now the Scottish people celebrate with glee! Mistletoe is hung in doorways to keep the evil spirits from entering the home.

On Christmas Eve, it's considered bad luck to allow a fire to go out. The custom reveals that only a burning fire will keep the elves from sliding down the chimney. Children hang their stockings in anticipate of see them filled when they wake up on Christmas Day. Santa is left a snack, such as mince pies, and a glass of milk (or a wee dram of whiskey) and the reindeer are treated to some carrots.

On Christmas day, people sometimes make big bonfires and dance around them to the playing of bagpipes. A person who is the first visitor to a home on Christmas Day is referred to as the First Footer. They must bring gifts of bread, money and peat to represent food, wealth and warmth to the household. (Later this has become a New Year's Day custom.) A long-standing tradition is to place candles in the window, to welcome and honor the visit of a stranger, such as Mary and Joseph who were searching for shelter.

Although Christmas celebrations have come out of the dark ages in Scotland, the largest celebration in Scotland is Hogmanay, the merriment of seeing in a New Year. Beginning on New Year's Eve and for the next week, the revelries include street festivals, parties, and fun filled bonfires to warm and brighten mid-winter. The fires are also an old Viking custom, used to end the old year and keep evil spirits away for the new year.

As previously mentioned First Footing is a common practice and starts the New Year with hospitality and good cheer. Another tradition is called "Redding the House." It might include burning pieces of juniper branches, where the smoke absorbs the bad spirits, then are blown away through open windows. This ritual removes the last year's bad luck and brings a fresh outlook for good luck in the new year.

Beloved Scottish poet Robert Burns wrote the lyrics to "Auld Lang Syne" in 1788, and used a Scottish folk song for the tune.

Robert Burns 1759-1796

It quickly became a custom to sing the song on Hogmanay or New Year's Eve, and as people from the British Isles emigrated around the world, the song gained the popularity it has today. In Scotland, people across the country gather and cross arms to share this world-renowned song in unison.

*Thanks to my dear friends, Robert and Jean Callahan, of Falkirk, Scotland, for their hospitality during my journey to their beautiful country. The extraordinary Robert Burns Dinner, complete with my first taste of Haggis, is a memory I cherish.

Dundee Cake ~

This traditional Christmas cake's been popular since the 19th century. A familiar story is that the Dundee cake was specially made without cherries for Mary Queen of Scots, who did not like cherries. It's similar to the American fruitcake and uses blanched almonds to decorate the top.

Ingredients ~

8 ounces flour

6 ounces butter

5 ounces granulated sugar

4 Eggs

1 ounce almonds

1 ½ ounces mixed fruit peel

6 ounces each currants, raisins, sultanas white raisins

Zest and juice of lemon

1 teaspoon baking powder

2 tablespoons whisky

2 Tablespoons boiled milk with 1 Tablespoon sugar

Directions ~

Blend the butter and sugar until creamy. One at a time, add the four eggs, plus a spoonful of flour with each egg, whisking as you add everything. Add the nuts and fruits. Sift the remainder of the flour with the baking powder and whiskey, then all to the other ingredients, stirring well. Add a little milk if the mixture is too stiff.

Preheat oven to 325F. Pour mixture in an 8-inch cake pan lined with parchment or well grease. Use your hands to push the mixture down flat. Cover with aluminum foil and bake for two hours. After one hour, remove the foil and place the split almonds in circles, waves or other design on the top. After two hours check to be sure the middle of the cake is cooked, and cook 10-15 extra minutes if necessary. Use the milk and sugar mixture to coat the top of the cake. After 15 minutes, remove the cake from the pan and cool on a wire rack. When cool, store the cake in a sealed container, but it does not have to be refrigerated. If desired, another tablespoon of whiskey can be pour over each slice of cake before serving!

Scotch Eggs ~

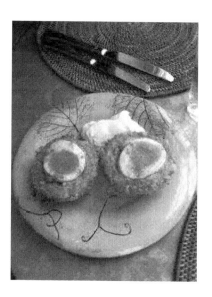

This is a traditional Scottish dish that is easy to make and great for an appetizer, breakfast, as a side dish, or for a picnic! It can be served hot or cold and stores well in the refrigerator for several days.

Ingredients ~

1 pound sausage meat

4 hard-boiled eggs, removed from shells

1 raw egg

3 ounces of dry breadcrumbs

1 teaspoon chopped thyme

1 Tablespoon chopped parsley

1 teaspoon Dijon mustard

Zest of 1 lemon

Pinch of salt and pepper

Small quantity of flour

1 Tablespoon water

Light oil such as canola oil, for frying

Directions ~

Combine the sausage, all spices, mustard, lemon zest, and salt and pepper and divide into 4 portions. Sprinkle flour on a surface and roll the shelled boiled eggs in the flour to lightly coat. Mold the sausage mixture all around the egg. Whisk the raw egg with water and coat the meat/eggs, then roll in the breadcrumbs, pressing them in all around. Carefully place the egg/meat balls into the hot oil and fry for 5-6 minutes. You can cook in a shallow pan, and turn often to make sure the meat is fully cooked. Allow to drain on a towel, then serve hot. The Scotch egg can also be cooled and eaten as a cold snack.

"Nollaig Chridheil!"

France

SINCE FRANCE IS bordered by Italy, Germany and Spain, Christmas celebrations are different according to the various regions and their neighbor's customs. Seasonal festivals are celebrated during the entire month of December, and traditions carry on into January and February! La fête de Saint Nicolas, is the beginning of the Christmas season in eastern and northern France on December 6.

Lyon, in southeastern France, has the festival of lights, Fête de lumières, on December 8. Residents put lighted candles in their windows to welcome the holy family.

In Bordeaux, in the southwestern region, a renowned Christmas village of wooden chalets sells local specialties including chocolate, Armagnac, and offerings from fine artists. On February 2, a feast to honor the Virgin Mary and baby Jesus is called Candlemas, or la Chandeleur, and celebrated by Catholics throughout the country.

Pere Noel is the name the French give to Santa. Saint Nicolas, or Sinterklass, distributes gifts on St. Nicholas Eve (December 6) and on Christmas Eve. Folklore tells of an evil "bogeyman," le Père Fouettard who takes care of the children who have been bad. Dressed in black and covered in coal dust, he accompanies Pere Noel on his journey as they discover who's been naughty or nice.

Thankfully, le Père Fouettard has all but disappeared, and other modern-day characters such as reindeer and elves are adored.

A nativity scene, or crèche, can be found in almost every home, and in decorations around every town and village.

Brightly colored figures call santons (little saints) involve great artisanship and molds to make the crèche figurines have been passed down since the 17th century. Many local villages have reenactment of the Christmas story with actors and with puppets.

A law was passed in France in 1962, stating that anyone sending a letter to Pere Noel would receive a response with a seasonal postcard. On Christmas Eve, the churches and cathedrals ring their bells and Christmas carols are sung in the streets. Christmas morning, children awaken to find Santa has filled their shoes, which were left by the fireplace, with small toys, sweets and nuts. Of course, carrots and hay was left for Santa's reindeer

After mass on Christmas Eve, Réveillon is the largest feast of the holiday and is a time for families to share the selection of the most luxurious and delectable foods of their region. The Réveillon dinner is a sacred custom, and is part of the French tradition to extend the time at the table, which can be as long as six hours. Le Réveillon is a reminder of the reason Christmas is celebrated and is a magical culinary experience for adults and children, whether celebrated in a home or an all-night restaurant. Delicacies such as oysters, lobster, foie gras, snails, venison, cheeses, frog's legs, scallops are enjoyed in a variety of dishes. Truffles and a chocolate sponge cake log called a bûche de Noël is a holiday tradition. The yule log shaped cake is often made of chocolate and decorated with extreme care to replicate an actual log. We've included a recipe for the log cake and other variations of the cake can be found online.

Buche de Noel or Yule Log Cake ~

Ingredients ~

Sponge cake ~

4 eggs

2/3 cup sugar

1 teaspoon vanilla

¼ teaspoon salt

1 cup cake flour

Directions ~

Preheat oven to 400 degrees. Line a 10 x 15 inch jellyroll pan with parchment paper. Spray the paper with cooking oil spray or brush with melted butter.

In a mixing bowl beat the eggs until they turn foamy. Add the salt, sugar, and sugar to the eggs and beat for 2 minutes. A few spoonful at a time, fold the flour into the egg mixture until all the flour is added. Do not over mix.

Smooth the batter into the pan. Bake for approximately 10 minutes, until the cake is set. Turn the cake on to a dry towel and remove the parchment paper. After about 3 minutes, gently roll the cake with the towel and allow to cool.

Chocolate buttercream ~

Ingredients ~

7 egg whites

1 1/3 cups granulated sugar

2/3 cup water

6 ounces unsweetened chocolate, melted

½ teaspoon instant espresso powder or instant coffee

½ teaspoon vanilla

3 cups plus 3 tablespoons butter, softened

Directions ~

Beat the egg whites in a dry bowl, until it forms soft peaks. Set aside.

Bring the water and sugar to a boil in a small saucepan, allowing it to thicken slightly. Keeping the beaten egg whites in their bowl, turn the blender on high and slowly pour the sugar syrup in with the eggs. Once that is incorporated, add the melted chocolate, espresso powder, and vanilla and continue blending until the mixture is cool. Stir the butter into the mixture, a few spoons at a time, until all the butter is included.

Assembling the Yule Log ~

Gently unroll the cake. Spread about 2 cups of the buttercream on the inside of the curve of the cake and form it into a roll. Trim off the ends of the roll and use the pieces to add to the center of the roll to make it look like a branch coming off the log.

Use the remaining frosting to cover the exterior of the log and branch. Use a small spatula or knife to make marks in the frosting to give it the look of tree bark. A sprig of holly can be added to the bark, or at the base of the cake to complete the holiday look.   Refrigerate before serving and chill any uneaten portion of the cake.

Ratatouille ~

Often called a "poor man's dish," Ratatouille comes from Nice, which is located in the southeastern area of France and borders the Mediterranean Sea. Made from a variety of vegetables such as tomatoes and zucchini, it can be served as a side dish but makes a hearty meal alone or served over rice. You may substitute the eggplant with one small butternut squash and alternate almost any of the vegetables to your liking!

Ingredients ~

2 eggplants, cut into cubes

2 zucchini, cut into slices

1 bell pepper (green, red, or yellow) cut up

5 tomatoes peeled and sliced (or 3 cans of diced tomatoes)

2 cloves garlic crushed

1 small white onion, sliced

2 sprigs rosemary

2 sprigs thyme

4 tablespoons olive oil, divided

3/4 teaspoon salt

1/4 teaspoon ground black pepper

2 tablespoons capers, drained (optional)

1/3 cup dry white wine

Directions ~

Preheat the oven to 375F. Toss all the vegetables in a large container with 2 tablespoons of olive oil. Place the vegetables in a large baking dish and roast the vegetables for 30-45 minutes, until they are brown around the edges. Transfer the vegetables into a large bowl, removing the springs of rosemary and thyme. Toss the roasted ratatouille with the remaining olive oil, wine, salt, pepper, and drained capers. Serve it warm or at room temperature with crusty French bread.

"Joyeux Noel!"

Mexico

THE LOVELY RED and green poinsettia plant, indigenous to Mexico, are a Christmas decoration staple in many areas of the world. It's well known English name is derived from Joel Roberts Poinsett, an American ambassador to Mexico, who brought the plant to the United States in 1825.

(Often mispronounced "poinsetta," the correct enunciation is poin-sett-i-a.) Mexican folklore tells the story of a young boy who had no gift to offer the baby Jesus. As he was placing the green branches at the church's nativity scene, the plant began to bloom the bright red flowers. Its star-shaped bloom is often compared to the Star of Bethlehem.

Mexicans celebrate Christmas with many long held traditions, which begin around the middle of December. Posadas is a very important celebration that encompasses the nine days before Christmas and ends on Christmas Eve. The nine days represent the nine months Mary carried Jesus and the nine days journey to Bethlehem.

During posadas groups of people visit different houses each of the nine nights, recreating the journey of Mary and Joseph searching for a place to rest. (In Spanish posada means "inn" or "shelter.")

There are often people who play the part of the holy couple, and the candles lighting their way is a beautiful image. The participants stop at the door and a traditional song is exchanged between the visitors and the host family. The desperate pleas of Joseph are hauntingly beautiful. Here are the poignant verses:

Joseph: *In the name of heaven, I ask you for shelter, for my beloved wife can go no farther.*

Host: *This is not an inn, Get on with you, I cannot open the door, you might be a rogue.*

Joseph: *Do not be inhuman; Show some charity, God in heaven will reward you.*

Host: *You may go now and don't bother us anymore because if I get angry I will beat you.*

Joseph: *We are worn out all the way from Nazareth, I am a carpenter named Joseph.*

Host: *Never mind your name, Let me sleep, I've already told you, we won't open the door.*

Joseph: *We request lodging, dear innkeeper, for only one night for the Queen of Heaven.*

Host: *Well if it's a queen who's asking why is it that she's out at night, wandering so alone?*

Joseph: *My wife is Mary. She is the Queen of Heaven; she will be mother to the Divine Word.*

Host: *Is that you Joseph? Your wife is Mary? Enter pilgrims I didn't recognize you.*

Joseph: *May the Lord reward you for your charity, and may the sky be filled with happiness.*

Host: *Happy home, harboring on this day the pure virgin, the beautiful Mary.*

(The doors are opened.)

All sing: *Enter holy pilgrims, pilgrims receive this corner not this poor dwelling but my heart.*

Tonight is for joy, for pleasure and rejoicing for tonight we will give lodging to the Mother of God the Son.

The host family then provides a fiesta where family and friends celebrate with traditional food, drink and games. The popular piñata is filled with Christmas candy and toys for the children to enjoy.

Nacimientos, Nativity crèches, are displayed in homes, yards and public areas starting on December 16, and on Christmas Eve, baby Jesus is added to the scene. On January 5, the three kings are included.

Pastorelas are great entertainment around the Christmas season. The performances began many years ago as a method to teach the Mexicans about Christianity. In Spanish Pastorela translates to "little shepherdess" and the biblical story portrayed shepherds visiting Jesus, confronted by angels and devils offering differing ways to go. Over time, the theatrical productions have become comedic, with a humorous view of the struggle between good and evil.

Christmas Eve, the last night of the posada, is called Nochebuena. Many Mexicans celebrate a midnight mass, called la Misa Del Gallo or "rooster's crow mass." The same name is given to the mass on New Year's Eve, to welcome a new beginning. Songs and lullabies are sung and families return home for dinner. Christmas Day is generally a quiet day. Gifts are not traditionally exchanged on Christmas, but this is changing, and Santa Claus is becoming increasingly more prominent in Mexican Christmas celebrations.

As in many countries, January 6 is Three Kings Day, or the Day of Epiphany, twelve days after Christmas. Dia de los Reyes is the time gifts are exchanged, celebrating the day The Three Kings visited the baby Jesus. A circular cake known as rosca de reyes, is a culinary custom throughout Mexico. It is similar to a fruitcake but it is flat and not as dense, and often contains a small toy Jesus. The person who receives the plastic figure is appointed to host the fiesta on Candlemas Day, February 2. Although these traditions are still actively practiced, Santa Claus bringing gifts has become more prominent in recent years.

February 2 is Día de la Candelaría, or Candlemas. This is the day Mexicans take down their decorations and nativity scenes but they take the Jesus figure to church to celebrate his birth. This finishes the Christmas season in Mexico.

Rosca de Reyes or Three Kings Cake ~

Some recipes use the candied fruit in the batter of the cake, and others use the fruit to decorate the top. This recipe bakes the fruit inside the cake AND on the top of the finished cake!

Ingredients ~

2 cups all-purpose flour

1 package active dry yeast

1 teaspoon salt

½ cup granulated sugar

1 teaspoon powdered cinnamon

¼ teaspoon nutmeg

¼ cup warm milk

4 Tablespoons butter

1 egg

1 teaspoon vanilla extract

1 cup candied fruit chopped ~ your choice of
cherries, pineapple, figs, orange, lime

(3/4 in cake and ¼ for topping)

¼ pecans, chopped

¼ cup dark rum or tequila

1 Plastic baby figurine (optional)

Egg Wash ~

1 egg

2 tablespoons water

Directions ~

Place all the candied fruit in a small bowl and add the rum or tequila, allowing it to soak for about 20 minutes. Whisk all the dry ingredients in a large bowl until blended. Add the fruit (3/4 cup) with the liquor, egg, butter, vanilla, and pecans. Stir well and then knead on a floured surface, forming a large ball. Cover bowl of dough with plastic wrap, and place in a warm area for 1 hour to allow the dough to rise.

Preheat oven to 350. Roll the raised dough on a floured surface to make a tube shape, and then bring the ends together to form a ring. If using the baby figurine, place it under the dough, or wait and push it into the cooked cake. Use cooking spray on a large cookie sheet and place the ring of dough on the sheet. Use the egg and water to make a wash for the top of the dough, then brush over the top of the cake. Use the remaining ¼ cup of fruit to decorate the top. Bake until golden brown, for about 45 minutes.

Ponche con Piquet or Punch with a Stin

Piquet is a seasonal punch with fruit and spices, and with a shot of rum, tequila or brandy, you can add the piquete, or sting. Some of the ingredients may not be readily available and use can substitute with other fruits.

1 gallon water

1 cup white sugar

1/2 pound dark brown sugar

2 cups raisins

1 1/2 pound of peeled sugar cane, peeled and cut into 1/4" julienne

2 large apples, roughly chopped

2 pears, roughly chopped

1/2 pound guavas, roughly chopped

2 pounds tejocotes

1 orange unpeeled, cut into quarters

1 small pineapple, peeled, cored and cut into chunks

4 or 5 cinnamon sticks

4 or 5 whole cloves (push into orange peel)

2 star anise

20 Jamaica flowers

Zest from one orange

In a large pot, heat the water. When the water is hot, stir in the white and brown sugars. Bring to a boil and make sure the sugar is dissolved. Put in the spices and fruit, reduce to a simmer and allow the flavors to blend for 30-60 minutes. During the last few minutes, add the zest of the orange. Serve warm with a shot of rum, brandy or tequila if desired. Refrigerate unused punch.

"Feliz Navidad!"

Russia

DURING MUCH OF the 20th century, Christmas was not celebrated in Russia and the "Festival of Winter" took its place. Suppressed by communism, religious observances did not have any importance in Russia, and those who believed in Christianity could not publicly celebrate. As resurgence in the return of religion acceptance occurred in the early 1990's, more and more people are beginning to enjoy the festivities of the Christmas season.   The primary religion is Russian Orthodox, and the honor the beliefs of the Christian community. As with other countries with Eastern Orthodox religions, Christmas is celebrated on January 7.

In December and January, Russia has temperatures that often fall below zero, and the country is covered with snow. This does not hinder the enthusiasm of the Russian citizens. Although the customs are a bit different, the main spirit of the season is the same. There are many rituals, folklore and Christmas characters in Russia, which are delightful.

Christmas traditions in Russia are similar to those in areas of Eastern Europe, where Orthodox Churches are prevalent. According to the Orthodox calendar, Russians honor Christmas on January 7, making Christmas Eve January 6. Members of the Orthodox Church attend services on Christmas Eve and many people fast for 39 days before the night. Later, when the first star appears in the sky, the dinner can begin. In the center of the table are a candle, representing Christ's light in the world, and "pagach," a special bread symbolizing Christ as the "bread of life." A white tablecloth and a bunch of hay denote Jesus' lowly beginnings. To honor the twelve apostles, there is a twelve-course dinner. There is fish, Borsch, stuffed cabbage, dried fruit and other delicacies.

Since New Year's Day precedes Russian Christmas on January 7, it is considered the more important holiday. In the spirit of worldwide unity, many Russians observe Christmas on December 25, and then New Year's is celebrated on January 14. The large Christmas tree, or "yelka" is decorated in Moscow's Red Square, serves as a nod to Christmas and the beginning of a New Year.

Babushka, which means "grandmother," is a character from a legend that's been carried through many generations. The story is told that Babushka did not want to go with the three wise men to see Jesus because it was too cold. Later she decided to go and filled a basket with gifts, but she was not able to find the manger and ended up visiting homes along the way and leaving the presents for the good girls and boys. Today the Babushka is a traditional symbol and is immortalized in the Russian "nesting dolls."

The Russian equivalent of Santa Claus is known as Grandfather Frost (Dedushka Moroz), or Father Frost (Ded Moroz.) The granddaughter of Grandfather Frost is Snegurochka, or Snowmaiden, and she always accompanies him on his journeys to bring presents to the children.

On New Year's Eve, children form a circle around the yelka (Christmas tree) and sing out to summon Snegurochka, and her father or grandfather. Ded Moroz appears carrying a magic staff, and when he waves it, the lights on the tree begin to twinkle!

Borscht ~

This traditional Russian soup is warm and hearty. It stores well and many claim it is better after a day or two!

Ingredients ~

3 medium potatoes, cut into cubes

½ head of cabbage, shredded

10 cups water

6 cups chicken broth

3 medium beets, washed and peeled, cut into small cubes (You can make this soup quicker by using canned beets, and include the juice.)

1 medium onion diced

2 carrots grated

4 Tablespoons oil

5 Tablespoons tomato sauce or ketchup

2 bay leaves

4 Tablespoon lemon juice

¼ teaspoon   ground pepper

1 teaspoon salt

2 Tablespoon chopped dill

1 can white beans with juice

Directions ~

In a large pot, add the water and chicken broth. Insert the cubed potatoes in the boiling liquid and cook for 15 minutes. Add the shredded cabbage and boil for 5 minutes.

Add olive oil to a large skillet at medium to high heat.   Sautée the beets (if using fresh), carrots, and onions for 10 minutes.   If using canned beets, stir them in with the vegetables and add the tomato sauce, when the other vegetables are almost finished. Lowering the heat, cook for 5 minutes, and then add everything in the skillet to the soup mixture. Add the lemon juice, salt, ground pepper, bay leaves, fresh dill and can of white beans, including liquid, to the soup pot. Cook 5-10 minutes, until you are certain the potatoes, beets and cabbage are soft. If desired, use additional salt and lemon juice. Serve hot with crusty bread.

Pierogi ~

This Russian specialty is a dumpling filled with a variety of stuffing, such as cheese, sauerkraut, or potatoes. Uncooked pierogies freeze well. Brush with melted butter to keep from sticking.

Ingredients for Sauerkraut Filling ~

2 Tablespoons vegetable oil

1 cup chopped onion

1 cup chopped mushrooms

14 ounces sauerkraut - drained, rinsed and minced

1/4 teaspoon salt

1/4 teaspoon ground black pepper

2 Tablespoons sour cream

Directions for filling ~

Heat the oil in a large pan on medium heat. Stir in the mushrooms and onions and cook until tender. Add sauerkraut, salt, and pepper and keep on heat for 8-10 minutes. After removing from heat, add sour cream. Set aside while making the peirogi dough.

Ingredients for dough ~

8 cups all-purpose flour

4 eggs

1 (8 ounce) container sour cream

1/2 teaspoon salt

Warm water

Directions for dough ~

Using a large mixing bowl, beat eggs, sour cream, and salt. Mix in the flour and warm water, a little at a time, until the dough is smooth. Place the dough on a floured surface, and knead. Use a rolling pin to press the dough into approximately ¼' thick. Use a cookie cutter or top of Mason jar to cut out 3-4 inch circles.

Spoon 1-2 tablespoons of sauerkraut filling on one half of the dough circle, then fold and press the edges to seal in the filling. Repeat until ingredients are used.   Use a large pot to bring water to a boil.   Gently place the pierogi in the boiling water, and remove it when it floats to the top.

"S Rozhdestvom!"

Australia

CHRISTMAS IN AUSTRALIA arrives in the middle of summer, where it can be 100 degrees (30 Celsius) on Christmas Day. It's winter, by the way, in the United States, for example, and of course it's December 25th in Australia (if 14 hours ahead of the U.S.), but the seasons are opposite. Outdoor activities at the beach like surfing, swimming, picnicking, and fishing are common. Bondi Beach near Sydney is a favorite spot for the holiday and it is not surprising to find that cold meats and salads are served for Christmas dinner.

During the summer in the "land down under", children are out of school and many offices are closed from Christmas Even to Australia Day on January 26. With so many people having time off, it's a great opportunity for families to get together and enjoy the extended holidays.

Despite the difference in the weather, Australians celebrate Christmas in much the same way as the rest of the world. Immigrants England and Ireland brought their holiday customs with them. Christmas trees and decorations are displayed, even using snowflakes and other symbols from colder climates are used. Many neighborhoods have competitions for the best decorations and most homes will have an adorned Christmas tree. Every year Sydney's Queen Victoria Building displays a tree containing over 60,000 lights and 15,000 Swarovski crystals.

There are many beautiful plants in bloom during the holiday season such as nasturtiums, wisteria, and honeysuckle. Australians decorate with the flora and fauna that is native to their area. Christmas Bushes are favorites for the season due to their small red-flowered leaves, as is the Christmas Bellflower with its red bells with golden tips.

When you think of the classic "white Christmas" and the frosty images portrayed on cards and advertisements, Christmas in Oz might seem a bit strange. Although Santa and his eight reindeer are not unheard of, many people in the Australian outback prefer the tradition of Santa's sleigh being pulled by his "six white boomers." A boomer is the universal icon for Australia, the kangaroo!

Traditional Christmas songs are enjoyed during gatherings and the Australian humor is revealed when they take a song like Jingle Bells and adapt it to their climate. Here's a portion of the song:

Jingle Bells, Jingle Bells

Jingle all the way

Christmas in Australian

On a scorching summer's day

Jingle Bells, Jingle Bells

Christmas time is beaut

Oh, what fun it is to ride

In a rusty Holden Ute.

(FYI ~ A Holden Ute is a car made in Australian by General Motors. Ute is short for "utility." It's much like Chevrolet's El Camino with two doors for passengers and a cargo bed like a truck.)

"Carols by Candlelight" is a popular tradition that began in 1937. It's held in open areas throughout Australia every evening during the week proceeding Christmas Day.

Families bringing picnics and folding chairs gather, rain or shine, to sing carols, while basking in the glow of thousands of candles. Aussies celebrate the theme of celebrating "peace on earth," which is a general feeling throughout the country.

Aborigines, Australia's indigenous people, number around 400,000 and make up approximately 2% of the population. The true

Aboriginal culture does not recognized Christianity, although they are very spiritual people in their own beliefs. Many aborigines who have incorporated the mainstream culture will celebrate Christmas with the rest of Australia.

Australian's Christmas dinner is much like American feasts. Roasted turkey and baked ham are served, with the insight to serving these in picnic sandwiches later when they go to the beach. Cold salads are plentiful, as are other items cooked on "the barbie" such as chicken wings and shrimp. Desserts have a great allure and most likely include the traditional "pavlova," trifles, Anzac biscuits, mince pies, plum puddings and chocolates. A plum pudding soaked in brandy is customary dessert fare.

As with their British and Irish cousins, Aussies celebrate Boxing Day on December 26. It's customary to show signs of gratitude to service people such as domestic help, the grocer, and the post person with a tip or gift. The day after Christmas is the day Australians joins in supporting their favorite teams playing cricket, and watching the Sydney to Hobart yacht race.

New Year's Eve celebrations are filled with parties and family gatherings. January 6, which is "Twelfth Night," the last party of the season takes place, bringing to a close the Christmas holidays.

Pavlova ~

This traditional dessert is basically a meringue shell with whipped topping and fruit. Meringue can be tricky so be sure the egg whites are at room temperature. After baking, they may deflate or crack. Just fill in the cracks with some extra whipped topping and fruit.

Ingredients ~

4 large egg whites *at room temperature*

1 cup of Castor sugar, or super fine granulated sugar

1 teaspoon of white vinegar

1/2 Tablespoon of cornstarch

1/2 teaspoon of pure vanilla extract

1/2 cups of whipping cream

Fresh fruit such as strawberries, raspberries, blackberries, kiwi, passion fruit, peaches, pineapple or blueberries. (Avoid bananas, as they will turn brown.)

Directions ~

Preheat oven to 275F. Line a cookie sheet with foil. Use a toothpick to draw a 7-8 inch circle in the foil, and then set aside.

Make sure to use a clean, dry metal bowl when adding the egg whites. Beat with an electric mixer on medium speed, until soft peaks are formed. One teaspoon at time, sprinkle the sugar in the egg whites, never stopping the beating until all the sugar is added. The egg whites should be stiff and glossy. Lightly add the cornstarch and vinegar to the egg whites, and fold very gently with a spatula. Include the vanilla and fold into the mixture.

Using the plastic spatula spread the meringue on the foil line sheet. Make sure it stays within the circle and that the outer edges are a bit higher that the middle, making a slightly indented area for the toppings to be added later. Bake for about 1 hour and 15 minutes. Leave the tray in the oven but turn off the heat and leave the door ajar to allow the meringue to cool. It will crack but don't worry as this can be covered. When the meringue is completely cool, remove it from the oven and pull off the foil before you turn it out on a nice serving plate.

Add a little vanilla extract to the whipping cream and beat until it forms peaks. (Prepared whipped cream can also be used.) Wash, clean and prepare the fruit in small pieces. Spread the whipped cream on top of the meringue, leaving an inch or two of the outer edge of the meringue showing. Put the fruit on top of the whipped cream, in a design or randomly. Enjoy!

Mango Lassi ~

Ingredients ~

2 mangos - peeled, stone removed and diced

2 cups low fat natural yoghurt

1/2 cup (125g) caster sugar

Ice cubes

Directions ~

Add everything in a blended and mix until smooth. Pour into glasses and serve. Easy breezy!

"G'day and Merry Christmas!"

Norway

NORWEGIAN CHRISTMAS CELEBRATIONS begin on December 13, with the Saint Lucia ceremony. According to tradition, at sunrise the youngest daughter from each family dons white robe with a red sash, and a crown of tall candles with an evergreens halo. Boys wear long white shirts and pointed hats to represent stars. The children wake their parents, and serve them a spiced bun called lussekatter and hot coffee. This custom begins the Christmas festivities in Norway. Church services feature the costumed group in choirs and village parades.

Many Norwegians decorate their Christmas trees on December 23, which is known as "little Christmas Eve." Julaften is Christmas Eve and the main day for celebrating Christmas and gathering for the holiday meal. In the afternoon, church bells call many people to the churches for religious services. In many villages, the bells ring again to announce the beginning of Christmas. Juledag, Christmas day, is often considered a day to spend quietly with family. On December 26, it is common to gather with friends, and finish the leftover food from Christmas Eve.

Christmas in Norway is filled with snow, and it has become the favorite holiday of the year. A magical mix of ancient fantasies and modern customs bring a lively spirit to the season. Nordic tribes were said to have burned the first Yule logs, to keep them warm through the chilling winder. Holly and ivy have been used for centuries to decorate the frosty doors and windows.

Norwegians have a tradition of hospitality even to strangers, and at Christmas time, it's amplified, to make certain that no one should be unhappy during the holidays. People utilize their time off work to visit family and friends during the season.

Julesnissen, or Santa Claus, is a Christmas gnome who brings the children presents.

Then there is Nisse, a gnome or an elf with goat features, who is the guardian of the animals. Children leave bowls of porridge for Nisse outside or even in the forest, or he might play tricks on them.

A "Julebukk" is a popular Christmas decoration that's made of straw. From Norse mythology, this goat drew the cart of the god of thunder, Thor. In Viking days, people use to cover themselves with a goatskin and lug a goat head around on the Christmas Day. In the time of early Christianity, this practice came to be linked to the devil, and the game was banned by the church. In modern day, the goat is used, but in the harmless, gentler version of Julebukk.

In 1947, Oslo delivered a beautiful Christmas tree to London, England in thanks for the assistance the British gave to Norway during World War II. The tree placed in Trafalgar Square is now an annual Christmas tradition.

The Stave Church in the village of Borgund is a classic image on Norwegian Christmas cards. The ancient church is replicated in Walt Disney World's EPCOT World Showcase, and is seen in the make believe village of Arendelle in the animated Disney movie, *Frozen.*

During noon on Christmas Eve, "lillejulaften," a porridge made from rice is traditionally served. There may be an almond in the porridge, and the one who finds it gets a small gift or maybe a treat, like a marzipan pig.

One of the most popular is a special bread called "Julekake" is a popular bread with raisins, candied peel and cardamom. Many Norwegians say that Christmas would not be Christmas without their favorite dish, "pinnekjøtt." "Lutefisk" a poached cod is also served to those with the acquired taste. Children love the red, sweet fizzy drink called Julebrus that is unique to Christmastime.

Adults might prefer beer or aquavit, Scandinavian liquor that's been produced since the 15th century. A favorite Christmas dessert is rice blended with whipped cream and served with a festive red sauce, and the simple to make Sand Kager cookies.

*Thanks to my dear friend and favorite Norwegian, Jonas Karlsen Astrom, for sharing his love of Norway.

Sand Kager ~

Ingredients ~

2 cups butter

2 cups sugar

1 cup finely chopped almonds

4 cups flour

Directions ~

Cream together the butter and sugar. With your hands, mix in flour and almonds. Press the mixture into a square baking tin and bake at 350 until golden brown. Cut into squares.

Farikal ~

This popular dish from Southern Norway combines lamb and cabbage, cooked with peppercorns.

Ingredients ~

8 ounces lamb meat

1 head cabbage

2 cups water

1 1/2 Tablespoons completely black peppercorns

Salt to taste

Directions ~

Place a layer of sliced lamb in the bottom of a soup pot. Put a layer of sliced cabbage on top of that and continue to layer until all the lamb and cabbage is in the pot. Put the peppercorns in a piece of cheesecloth and tie the top tightly. Place the bag in the pot and pour water in the water. Cover the pot and bring to a boil. Reduce heat and simmer on low for 2 hours. Take out the bag of peppercorns and serve with boiled potatoes or alone.

Pinnekjott ~

This dish requires mutton/sheep ribs, which have been dried. I've included this very basic recipe for those who are as curious as I was about this favorite Norwegian dish.

Ingredients ~

Slab of ribs, dried

Birch sticks

Instructions ~

Cut dried ribs apart and soak in cold water for 24 hours. Place clean sticks of birch (bark removed) in the bottom of a large pot. Put in the ribs and cover with water. Boil slowly, checking water level periodically. Cook for 2-3 hours or until tender. Serve with boiled potatoes and turnips.

"God Jul!"

Hawaii

United States of America

IF YOU ARE lucky enough to find yourself in Hawaii during the Christmas holidays, you will discover a unique and magical view of other American customs. Hawaiians have a celebration that begins four months before Christmas called Mahahiki. People of the islands honor mother earth with traditional rituals and feasts throughout this period. Custom states that all strife is forbidden during Mahahiki and the spirit of the season culminates when Christmas Day arrives. It's the definitive ending to months of celebration.

Missionaries introduced Hawaiians to Christianity and before then, the people of the islands did not celebrate Christmas. In 1786, Captain George Dixon arrived via ship on the island of Kauai on Christmas day.

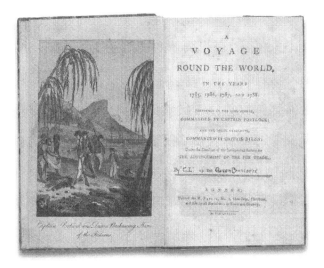

He wanted a dinner and celebration for his crew and he took the festivities ashore, making this Hawaii's first recorded Christmas. Hawaiians began their own celebrating of the season around 1820.

Festivities might vary between the Hawaiian Islands, but they all enjoy the Christmas season with enthusiasm. On the island of Maui, thousands of lights are scattered throughout Lahaina's Banyan Court, and a tree-lighting ceremony brings out residents and tourists alike to bask in the glow. With its Festival of Lights, the island of Kauai features a ceremony to light the Historic County Building and Royal Palm trees. The Lights on Rice parade, closes down Rice Street during this popular event. It's always the first Friday in December and there are over 50 fantastically lighted floats, marching bands and costumed performers to delight the crowds.

Carols are sung by all and Santa makes his grand

entrance.

The state capitol of Hawaii, Honolulu, is on

the island of Oahu and the majority of the

activities and seasonal sights are happening in this

city with the most tourism. "Honolulu Lights"

begin the first week of December and twinkle

through New Year's Day. The lighting of the 50-

foot pine tree in front of city hall is a highlight of
the festivities. A light parade follows and trolley
rides carry folks around to see the city aglow. At
the city hall's plaza fountain there's a huge
sculpture of Santa and Mrs. Claus in their
traditional Hawaiian clothes.

Santa Claus in Hawaiian is "Kanakaloka." Of
course a velvet Santa suit with fur trim would be

too hot for the tropical weather so Santa wears an aloha shirt and shorts, and goes barefoot! That makes sense because his "sleigh" is an outrigger canoe and it might be pulled by a team of dolphins. If the dolphins are not available, a team of paddlers will gladly escort Santa and his bag of gifts to greet the children on the beach! (The elves also wear aloha shirts.)

Hawaiians listen to traditional Christmas music but they have a few that are unique to their customs. The most well known Christmas song is "Mele Kalikimaka," which has been recorded by Bing Crosby, Bette Midler, Jimmy Buffet and many others including Hawaii's native son, Don Ho. A fun song written by three friend in their Diamond Head home in 1959 is called "12 Days of Christmas Hawaiian Style." We've included the last verse, which contains the "gifts" for all twelve days. (By the way, Tutu means Grandmother.)

Numbah Twelve day of Christmas, my tutu give to me

Twelve television, eleven missionary, ten can of beer,

Nine pound of poi, eight ukulele, seven shrimp a-swimmin',

Seex hula lesson, five beeg fat peeg,

Foah flowah lei, tree dry squid, two coconut,

An' one mynah bird in one papaya tree!

(Listen to this lively song on this YouTube link: https://www.youtube.com/watch?v=gc1WKCMXagU)

Traditional fir or pine Christmas trees do not grow in Hawaii but there is enough demand that trees are shipped in from various countries. Families who don't get a real tree for their homes decorate palm trees and other areas of their homes and yards in Hawaiian style. Poinsettias, which bloom at Christmas time, grow naturally in the tropical climate. They are not small plants in containers, but bushes that can grow as big as trees.

Many different ethnic groups make up the population of the islands, creating a vast array of traditions, which may be secular or religious. The warm weather and the beauty of Hawaii encourage the exchange of leis, beach activities, including the popular luaus, hula dancing, singing and the distinctively tropical ukulele.

Often communities and church groups celebrate Christmas with a kalua pig, a whole pig cooked in an underground oven called an imu. Sweet potatoes will include locally grown pineapples, as the favorite pineapple upside-down cake, with cherries to add a Christmas touch. A traditional Hawaiian pudding is made with coconut and for the holidays, might be layered with pumpkin. Real Hawaiian flowers are used to garnish dishes and decorate cakes and fruity drinks, complete with fresh tropical fruit on the rim. These little touches are the why the customs of Hawaiian life are like the rainbows often seen around the islands - magical and full of color!

Kalua Pork in a Crock Pot ~

Ingredients ~

5 pounds pork butt or shoulder

1 Tablespoon liquid smoke, teriyaki sauce or soy sauce

2 crushed garlic cloves

3 Tablespoons sea salt

Directions ~

Make cuts into the pork, and then rub all the surfaces with salt, garlic and liquid smoke or other seasoning. Seal in an airtight container and marinate overnight in the refrigerator. Place pork and juice in a crockpot and add one inch of water. Cook on low for 10 hours, turning pork over after

5 hours. Remove and put on a platter. Pork will easily shred apart. The pork is great on a toasted bun or served with some coleslaw.

Haupia ~

A staple for luaus, these can be cut into cubes, to enjoy a custard treat that is filled with the coconut favors of Hawaii.

Ingredients ~

2 16 ounce cans of Coconut Milk

3 cups water

16 ounces Cornstarch

1 cup granulated Sugar

Directions ~

Use 2 cups of water and mix with the cornstarch. Set to the side.

In a medium saucepan on high heat, combine the remaining 1 cup water, all of the sugar and coconut milk and bring to a rolling boil.

Add the cornstarch water into the coconut mixture and boil until it thickens, stirring constantly with a whisk. When the contents are thick and smooth, pour into a container around 9 x 11. Allow to cool then refrigerate and serve cold by cutting custard into 1" squares.

Blue Hawaiian Cocktail ~

Ingredients ~

1/2 ounce blue curacao

2 ounces light rum

1 ounce fresh pineapple juice

1 teaspoon coconut cream

Directions ~

Pour all ingredients into a shaker with ice. Strain and serve in a martini glass, rimmed with sugar.

"Mele Kalikimaka!"

Merry Christmas!

Merry Christmas from Zu!

And from Rodney and family!

What did you think?

Was this a fun read?

We really hope you liked *Christmas Around the World!* If you did, you might also like to have our book, *Thanksgiving Around the World and in Your Home.* You can get it now on Amazon!

Bimini Books

In fact, the publisher, Bimini Books, is always working to bring you engaging, light, fun and informative books. More are added all the time. To find out about the latest releases and events, please visit Bimini Books online and sign up for updates!

www.BiminiBooks.com

Your Honest Opinion

And as you may know, about the greatest gift you can give a writer (besides buying his or her book of course) is leaving an honest, useful review for *Christmas Around the World* on Amazon. *Thank you, in advance!*

About the Authors

Zu Barnes

WRITING UNDER THE pen name of Zu Barnes, Susan J. Z. Barnes resides near her roots of Northwest Florida's Emerald Coast. She grew up in Pensacola and has most recently called Destin, Florida, home. Susan enjoys spending time with her two adult children, Teresa and Daniel, and her two beloved grandchildren, Ethan and Skye. Her sister, Joni, is her inspiration and travel companion. An international traveler, Susan has visited Europe several times and frequently cruises to the Caribbean. When not traveling or visiting friends and family, Susan also enjoys a simple life at home with her two dogs, Zuzu and Mimzy.

Susan has loved to write for as long as she can remember and is excited to fulfill her dream of creating stories and poetry. During her lifetime, Susan has had many interesting adventures and experiences, in addition to different career opportunities. She most fondly cherishes the 11 years she was a Walt Disney World cast member, and special friend of Cinderella's Fairy Godmother. Susan now works from home, where she is writing a novel and dreaming of her next adventure!

You may contact Susan at Zubarnes@aol.com.

Rodney Miles

RODNEY IS THE author of over 50 works of fiction and non-fiction as a ghostwriter, and of over just as many as founder and CEO of Rodney Sanger and Associates, a Florida-based ghostwriting and self-publishing assistance firm. Rodney is also founder and CEO of Bimini Books, bringing you enjoyable lifestyle titles to escape and enjoy with.

Christmas has always played an important role in Rodney's life and was always looked forward to with anticipation, in fact Rodney hosts the family get-together and pondering international dishes to serve this year sparked the idea for this book.

Upcoming titles include *365 Surprising and Inspirational Rock Star Quotes.* Reach Rodney by email at <u>writingbyrodneymiles@gmail.com</u>.

References

- http://answerparty.com/question/answer/how-much-money-is-spent-in-the-united-states-at-christmas-time
- http://www.thehistoryofchristmas.com/traditions/italy.htm
- http://goitaly.about.c¬om/od/christmasinitaly/a/christmas.htm
- http://fisheaters.com/customsadvent7.html
- http://www.italylogue.com/planning-a-trip/italy-in-december.html
- http://britishfood.about.com/od/christmas/p/boxingday.htm
- http://www.worldholidaytraditions.com/Countries/England.aspx
- http://resources.woodlands-junior.kent.sch.uk/customs/xmas/santa.html
- http://www.dgreetings.com/gift-ideas/christmas-gifts/royal-christmas-message.html
- Clive and Gail Windley, Margate, Kent, England, UK
- http://www.timeanddate.com/holidays/ireland/st-stephen-day
- http://britishfood.about.com/od/maincours2/
- http://www.thehistoryofchristmas.com/traditions/scotland.htm

- http://www.worldofchristmas.net/christmas-world/scotland.html
- http://christmas.lovetoknow.com/Scottish_Christmas_Traditions
- http://www.rampantscotland.com/recipes/blrecipe_dundee.htm
- http://en.wikipedia.org/wiki/Dundee_cake
- http://www.frenchmoments.eu/christmas-in-france/
- http://frenchfood.about.com/od/desserts/r/Chocolate-Buche-De-Noel-Recipe.htm
- http://whychristmas.com/cultures/mexico.shtml
- http://www.santas.net/mexicanchristmas.htm
- http://gomexico.about.com/od/christmas/a/posada-song_2.htm
- http://spanglishbaby.com/food/traditional-rosca-de-reyes-3-kings-cake-recipe/
- http://chowhound.chow.com/topics/465889
- http://goeasteurope.about.com/od/russianculture/a/russiachristmastraditions.htm
- http://www.santas.net/russianchristmas.htm
- http://natashaskitchen.com/2012/03/16/borscht-recipe-ii/
- http://www.santaswarehouse.com.au/history_of_christmas/christmas_in_australia.shtml
- http://australianfood.about.com/od/bakingdesserts/r/Pavlova.htm
- http://allrecipes.com.au/recipe/1705/mango-lassi.aspx?o_is=Hub_TopRecipe_2

- http://www.theholidayspot.com/christmas/wor
ldxmas/norway.htm
- http://whychristmas.com/cultures/norway.sht
ml
- http://www.sofn.com/norwegian_culture/sho
wRecipe.jsp?document=Pinnekjott.html
- http://www.allthingschristmas.com/traditions/
christmas-hawaii.html
- http://www.ehow.com/how_11719_celebrate-
hawaiian-christmas.html
- http://www.polynesia.com/haupia.html#.VGa
a_Gd0zX4
- https://www.youtube.com/watch?v=gc1WKC
MXagU

Made in the USA
San Bernardino, CA
20 November 2017